PIECES OF PEACE

Every Piece of the Puzzle Promises a Peace of Mind

Anthony KaDarrell Thigpen &
THE AUTISM ACADEMY
For Education & Development

Literacy

The Autism Academy

For Education and Development

7541 S. Willow Drive
Tempe, AZ 85283
Phone: 480.347.9492
Fax: 480.718.8518
Autismacademyed.com

Laura Newcomb, *owner*

"Every Child is Exceptional"

Published by Literacy in Motion
Anthony_thigoen@aol.com

Anthony KaDarrell Thigpen editorial services, a subsidiary of Literacy in Motion.

Library of Congress Cataloging-in-Publication Data Publisher and Printing by Literacy in Motion Cover Design by Literacy in Motion Design Team

PIECES OF PEACE,
Every Piece of the Puzzle Promises a Peace of Mind
ISBN: 978 – 0 – 692 – 83334 - 6

Educational
Self-Help
Printed in the United States of America

"EVERY CHILD IS EXCEPTIONAL."

Proceeds from your purchase of this book will help promote autism awareness.

Special thanks from,

Laura Newcomb

THE AUTISM ACADEMY
For Education and Development

TABLE OF CONTENT

CONTENT *Continued*

UNDERSTANDING DIFFERENT BEHAVIORS

Stages of Stigmatism, Shame,
Embarrassment, and Denial

AUTISM ACADEMY – Shawn Davis is an experienced principal that was clueless concerning her own child's struggle with autism for 10-years.

Despite earning a Bachelor's degree in Elementary Education from Augusta State and a Master's from Cambridge College, identifying signs of autism requires a specialized skillset.

For years, the Muncie, Indiana elementary school principal says she thought her son had disciplinary issues.

However, no matter how much she lectured him, despite harsh punishments, and regardless of social consequences, nothing changed, she explained.

"Many teachers have no idea what to do with (undiagnosed) high functioning kids with autism," Davis explained. "It's a different dynamic from ordinary disciplinary issues."

Initially, autism behavior can lead to public shame and embarrassment because of associated stigmatisms.

Her son, like many others, learned how to blend in amongst other students and pretend when necessary to fit in with his classmates, According to Davis.

"Until I had the responsibility of sitting in on Individual Educational Plan (IEP) meetings, I didn't think my son's behavior was a big deal," she said. "Afterward, I scheduled a meeting with my son's school principal and requested a full battery of testing for autism."

She says when parents are in denial it only hurts the child in the end.

The test results were conclusive – Davis' son was diagnosed with autism spectrum disorder (ASD).

At that moment, she embodied an undying passion to advocate for students with autism.

Davis is amongst a growing population of parents.

Currently, according to the Centers for Disease Control and Prevention (CDC),

1-in-68 children are diagnosed with ASD – and the numbers are increasing rapidly.

As a result, it's important for parents to learn how to navigate the system to avoid unwanted abuse, as opposed to ignoring the signs.

Children with autism, especially those who slip through the cracks without a proper diagnosis, are often misunderstood and mistreated.

"That's why I'm determined to be an advocate for these kids," Davis said. "I plan to give them the tools and strategies they need in order to maintain in this society."

She relocated 2000 miles from Munsey, Indiana to Arizona to work as the principal for the Autism Academy in Peoria.

The specialty school has 72 students from grades K-9, 5 classrooms, and 26 caring teachers and attentive staff members.

Newcomers are encouraged to tour the school.

Davis and her staff raise awareness, empowering parents to cope with skepticism and unnecessary embarrassment.

They also go through extra measures to help new families adjust to their school environment.

Children with autism seldom succeed in mainstream general education classrooms. Some school districts do a great job including kids and adapting curriculum to meet special needs.

Unfortunately, most schools do a miserable job identifying autism and working with such students with dignity thereafter.

Even worse, children with autism are often targets for bully activity.

While there are pros and cons to private and public autism programs, Davis is positioned in the perfect place to fulfill her passion.

At the Autism Academy she's helping parents best educate their children with special needs.

In addition, she's enabling parents to understand how to identify autistic behavior from misbehavior, and how to handle both.

Autism affects 1 in 68 children, and boys are more likely to have autism than girls.

Quick Fact

Information provided by the CDC &
THE AUTISM ACADEMY
For Education and Development

AUTISM SPECTRUM SCREENING

Constitutional Rights Critical at Autism Academy

AUTISM ACADEMY – Diagnosing *Autism Spectrum Disorder* (ASD) can be difficult, since there is no medical test, like a blood screening, to diagnose the disorder.

The American Psychiatric Association's Diagnostic and Statistical Manual (DSM) provides standardized criteria to help professionals accurately diagnose the condition.

Pediatricians often look at the child's behavior and development to make a diagnosis.

ASD can sometimes be detected at 18 months or younger.

By age 2, a diagnosis by an experienced professional is usually considered very reliable.

However, many children do not receive a final diagnosis until much older.

This delay means that children with an ASD might not immediately get the help they need.

Diagnosing ASD can be approached three ways, a developmental screening, a comprehensive diagnostic evaluation, or an educational assessment.

Developmental screening is a short test to tell if children are learning basic skills when they should, or if they might have delays.

During this type of screening the doctor will likely ask the parent(s) some questions.

In addition, the physician usually interacts with the child to assess learning, speaking patterns, behaviors, and movement.

A delay in any of these areas could be a sign for concern.

All children should be screened for developmental delays and disabilities during regular well-child doctor visits at ages 9, 18, 24 or 30 months.

Additional screening might be needed if a child is at high risk for developmental problems due to reasons posed at birth.

According to Centers for Disease Control and Prevention, all children should be screened, specifically for ASD during regular well-child doctor visits at 18 or 24 months.

Even still, additional developmental screening might be needed.

If your child's doctor does not routinely check, you should ask for a developmental screening.

If the doctor sees any signs of a problem, a comprehensive diagnostic evaluation is needed.

The second type of diagnosis is the comprehensive evaluation.

This thorough review includes looking at the child's behavior, learning, speaking patterns, movement, social development, and interviewing the parent(s).

Comprehensive examines may also include hearing and vision screenings, genetic, neurological, and other medical testing.

In certain comprehensive cases, primary care doctors refer children to specialist like developmental pediatricians, child neurologists, or child psychologists.

An educational assessment is the third type.

This happens at local school districts based on the eligibility category under the *Individuals with Disabilities Education Act* (IDEA).

However, a medical diagnosis and educational assessments have different purposes.

The medical diagnosis is made to determine treatment strategy, advise future expectations, allow data collection and statistical analysis, and support billing of third-party payers.

On the other hand, an educational assessment is designed to determine eligibility for special educational assistance only.

It is important to note that each state sets its own assessment standards and procedures, within the limits of the IDEA.

However, many children assessed as autistic by the schools do not meet the DSM criteria for autism.

The Autism Academy for Education and Development upholds the 9 basic steps of IDEA:

1. The child is identified as potentially requiring special education support;

2.   The Child is Then Evaluated;
3.   After evaluation, the eligibility is determined;
4.   An Individualized Education Program (IEP) meeting is scheduled;
5.   The IEP is Written;
6.   The plan is carried out – services are provided;
7.   Ongoing measurement of progress and reporting to parents;
8.   The IEP is reviewed; and
9.   A re-evaluation is completed.

Administrators at the Autism Academy work hard to make sure that parents know their rights and children are properly tested.

Autism greatly varies from person to person, no two people with autism are alike.

Quick Facts

Information provided by the CDC &
THE AUTISM ACADEMY
For Education and Development

NEWLY DIAGNOSED?

Autism Academy Weighs in on Web-Based Information

AUTISM ACADEMY – Having a child that is newly diagnosed with Autism Spectrum Disorder (ASD) is stressful for some parents.

Upon receiving an initial diagnosis there are some important steps caregivers can make to help lighten the load.

All information is not reliable.

With the right support network, caring parents can empower their children to develop the skills needed to fully participate in family, school and community.

The process starts by reaching out to a specialty school where children with autism are able to flourish.

The Autism Academy offers proven individual education plans for the best possible results that help relieve your stress and nourish your child's development.

The plan helps parents with a reasonable and realistic approach for recently diagnosed children.

The step-by-step process starts with securing an individual educational plan, addressing physical concerns, and accommodating social needs.

Internet information is not always the best because oftentimes it is not based on solid scientific facts and findings.

Generic information about ASD treatment is made readily available for parents online.

Sifting through symptoms, situations and scenarios site-after-after intimidates many parents of newly diagnosed students.

However, parents dealing with this new diagnosis need face-to-face encounters, proven resources, and reliable professionals.

This is why the Autism Academy is positioned in various locations throughout the Phoenix region.

The team of teachers, administrators, speech pathologists, counselors, transition specialists, and other specialty professionals are helping parents lay aside unnecessary stress.

The Autism Academy internet blog is a great resource for general information that serves as a bridge connecting parents to professionals.

It's important for parents to gain more specific recommendations during personal onsite meetings where you and your child are able to learn necessary details.

"At the Autism Academy for Education and Development, we strive to improve the lives of each student, their families, and communities," said school founder and owner Laura Newcomb. "As a school focused on children with Autism, we achieve this by addressing the needs of every student academically, socially, and behaviorally."

The philosophy of the Autism Academy is to provide a solid foundation utilizing strategic-hands-on programs that build character and social skills. As a result, every student becomes a valued, productive, and successful person. The ultimate goal is to enrich and empower students to reach their highest potential and contribute to their communities by providing the best education possible.

The philosophy is accomplished by implementing compassionate character components designed to teach students strategies for Anti-Bullying and strong values.

The internet is often the plug-in point for most parents, but the Autism Academy is where education and development begins.

About 40% of children with autism do not speak. About 25-30% have some words at 12-18 months of age and then lose them. Others might speak, but not until later in childhood.

Quick Facts

Information provided by the CDC &
THE AUTISM ACADEMY
For Education and Development

LAURA NEWCOMB'S JOURNEY

New Narrative Advancing Education at Autism Academy

AUTISM ACADEMY – Laura Newcomb is building academic bridges, meeting social needs, and making education for children with autism more meaningful.

Her passion for helping people and meeting needs started decades before she opened the doors as founder of the Autism Academy in 2013.

Before completing her Bachelor's program at the University of Wyoming in 1988, she met the-late Donald Newcomb.

The *Elementary Education* and *Industrial Engineer* undergrads fell in love – August 11, 1990 the college sweethearts shared wedding vows.

Soon after, the Newcomb's built a family, giving birth to three children; Graham, 23, Kalona, 22, and Kalina, 19.

In 2002, the family relocated to Arizona.

Laura Newcomb continued her education at the University of Phoenix, earning a Master of Science in Administration, and a certification in Cross Categorical (Special Education).

Donald Newcomb earned a Master of Business Administration in Information Technology.

While working as a special education director, one of Laura's responsibilities included child placement.

"Most facilities would only take kids with an IQ of 90 or above," she said. "And no program worked with students only diagnosed with autism."

She noticed an unsupervised lower functioning student sitting under a lunchroom table at a private facility.

She describes that incident as the last straw that compelled the couple to develop a program that would teach and treat children with autism with dignity, compassion, and respect.

"The Autism Academy was birthed out of a need," she said.

Laura and Donald Newcomb merged their passions to support students with Autism with the dream of building amazingly unique schools.

They shaped a business plan, searched for investors, and secured a location. After conquering a lengthy process that included defining a specialized curriculum, the school attained accreditation.

"We started with 1 location, 24 students and 4 teachers," Newcomb said. "Now we have 3 locations, 120 employees, and 270 students."

On November 12, 2015, after a 25-year journey, the Newcomb family experienced a great loss – Donald died.

Laura's fingers remain on the pulse of the vision, passion and legacy that they gave birth to upon opening the doors of the Autism Academy.

The school continues to thrive and advance.

Newcomb says her source of success, strength and steadfastness comes from the secret of relying on her faith.

Despite personal challenges, she remained focused.

"We have an intense program," she said. "And we manage to attract good-hard-working professionals."

Unlike similar facilities, the Autism Academy covers the complete spectrum of different functioning levels of students with autism.

"We have a better system," Newcomb explained. "We will challenge any program in the area."

She described her ultimate school strategy as a system of putting kids first.

"I've always cared about helping people," she said. "And our innovative program is breaking barriers wherever the system needs change.

Currently, Newcomb's sites are set on launching an Autism Academy in Tucson,

Arizona because of regional need and repeated requests.

"Laura is selfless," said Peoria Autism Academy principal Shawn Davis. "She is a leader that I aspire to be like."

Others echoed similar sentiments.

She's supported by an assiduous executive team solving systemic

21

problems.

Her teachers and staff understand the importance of duplicating successful strategies and advancing academic excellence through quality programming and professionalism.

Newcomb is intentionally defining a new narrative that is rapidly advancing education for children with autism throughout Arizona.

The rate of autism has steadily grown over the last twenty years.

Quick Facts

Information provided by the CDC &
THE AUTISM ACADEMY
For Education and Development

6-STEP ENROLLMENT
Registration Process for Autism Academy

AUTISM ACADEMY – Enrollment coordinator Catelyn Foster uses an easy-to-follow 6-step registration process for parents seeking the best placement for children with autism.

STEP #1 The Tour

During an initial campus visit, parents and caregivers are escorted on a guided tour of the facility.

Guests are able to meet and observe teachers and staff, view classroom layouts, cafeteria/gymnasium, and examine our sensory room.

"Our sensory room has weighted blankets and vests that stimulate children with autism to help them feel better," Foster explained. "Oftentimes they need to feel pressure, some students temporarily need deem lighting, and sometimes we have to help them deal with taste and touch."

The school strategy of keeping kids first is well-measured from classroom layouts to curriculum choices.

STEP #2 Curriculum Overview

"Students rotate through various tables working with academics on their individual levels," Foster described. "We also have physical education, music, and art."

The Autism Academy uses MobyMax software to find and fix learning gaps by identifying strengths and weaknesses.

In addition, students participate in an explorer program every Friday that helps with transition beyond high school.

"This gives students with autism exposure to diverse career paths," she said.

Explorer course electives include cooking, robotics, coding and much more.

The school offers both non-traditional and conventional curriculums combined.

The school offers something for the entire family.

Parents participate in after-school Zumba classes with students in Tempe and parent specialty classes at all 3 sites.

STEP #3 Questions and Answers

"Many parents have unanswered questions and lingering concerns," Foster said. "We welcome parents and guests to ask specific questions and convey their concerns."

The Autism Academy accommodates students with behavioral challenges, specialized scheduling, and special needs rehabilitation.

Parents are also able to get *respite care* for adults in need of planned or emergency support.

Many parents also inquire about funding.

STEP #4 Special Needs Scholarships

Students diagnosed with autism qualify for the Empowerment Scholarship Account (ESA) or Student Tuition Organizations (STOs).

"You can apply for multiple STOs," said Foster. "But it has to be an ESA or STOs – one or the other."

An ESA is a year-round scholarship account similar to a checking account.

ESA transfers 90% of the state funding from the school your child previously attended to your school of choice.

Students with autism who qualify for the ESA program are able to attend the Autism Academy.

The remainder of the tuition is waived and ESA funding is accepted as full tuition.

STOs are not as clear cut as an ESA.

"STOs are private organizations offering tuition-based scholarships," Foster explained. "We prefer an ESA, but we help parents with the application process of their choice."

25

However, STOs have maximum allowances, they have no guaranteed funding year-after-year, and each STO requires a separate application process."

STEP #5 Student Assessment

Under the Individuals with Disabilities Education Act (IDEA), there are 13 categories under which a student is eligible for protection and services administered by law.

Examples include Other Health Impairments (OHI), Emotional Disturbance (ED), Speech Language Impairment (SLI), Specific Learning Disability (SLD), Traumatic Brain Injury (TBI), and Autism (A).

Educators use a Multiple Disciplinary Educational Team Report (MET) as a series of tests and evaluations to determine disability eligibility.

"We use the MET report to create an Individual Education Plan (IEP)," Foster said. "Sometimes it's difficult to get an autism diagnoses because it comes down to funding."

She says students diagnosed with autism have higher academic demands, require more services, and create added cost to schools.

Students with autism may need an array of services like occupational therapy, speech therapy, and one-on-one para-professionals.

As a result, a wide range of autism case studies indicate that many students with autism go undiagnosed.

"When you take the time and initiative to get involved you can avoid unwanted frustrations," Foster said. "It starts by knowing your own kid."

STEP #6 THE APPLICATION PROCESS

The final step is to apply.

Foster says the staff helps parents with the application from start to finish.

"We usually complete the ESA and Autism Academy applications in the same sitting," she said. "Parents only need an updated MET report and a birth certificate."

Academy administrators understand that the scholarship and enrollment applications are nerve-racking responsibilities for the most parents.

As a result, a special enrollment coordinator makes the process flow quickly and easily at the Autism Academy.

Once the application process is complete, approvals usually take less than 30-60 days.

Afterward, children will grow and learn from well-trained teachers who take pride in their students.

Staffers with specialized training in instruction and curriculum cater to students with autism in smaller class sizes.

Most importantly, student at the Autism Academy are surrounded with like-minds, a challenging environment, and a bully-free community of achievers.

Undecided parents are urged to apply immediately, because there is limited space available at the rapidly growing Autism Academy.

Children with autism do progress – early intervention is key.

Quick Facts

Information provided by the CDC &
THE AUTISM ACADEMY
For Education and Development

MOM MAKING DECISIONS

Operations Director Discovers Purpose at Autism Academy

AUTISM ACADEMY – Meet Jenny Durant, the Operations Director at Autism Academy, a school that provides an education for children with autism.

Jenny Durant was 18-years-old when she started making decisions that would impact others. 26 year later, as a wife, mother, and now operations director at the Autism Academy her methods have proven successful.

The specialty school takes pride in employing about 100 professional educators that work together under an invisible "kids first" banner. Before the school opened, Durant's decisions played a key role in helping to produce a proficient and peaceful work environment.

Her unexpected journey as a mom awarded her the experience needed to make the kind of decisions parents respect, students embrace, and teachers value. An unplanned pregnancy caused her to make some rapid choices at age 18. Durant said, "I had to quit living life like there was no tomorrow."

She married her high school sweetheart, Chuck Durant and started planning for their family. "I could no longer just be care-free," Durant said. "This was a huge wake-up call for me."

As a homemaker, she maneuvered the maze of household responsibilities, raising children, school volunteerism, church involvement, and being a wife. She bypassed the traditional college experience.

Instead, Durant discovered new friendships with older church congregants that provided priceless wisdom used to nourish a wholesome family and lasting marriage. In 2002, Durant decided to enter the workforce – as if raising four children wasn't enough. "I was able to stay home when my kids were younger, but as they got older I started thinking about what I wanted to do," she said. "Initially, I worked in retail." It wasn't long before she negotiated an administrative assistant position at her son's school. While working at Leading Edge Academy, Durant met 6th-grade teacher Laura Newcomb.

Newcomb possessed a passionate interest in helping unique learners, which launched her from the classroom to the director of special education. When Newcomb landed her first principal position at a nearby location, Durant packed her desk supplies and assumed duties as Newcomb's dedicated assistant. It doesn't stop there, by 2005, they were an inseparable cohort.

"That's when Laura (Newcomb) started Exceptional Academic Services," Durant said. "The new business contracted special education services to charter schools."

In 2013, Newcomb launched the Autism Academy, a school for children with autism.

Durant contributed decisions that helped make the specialty school the fastest growing in the region, working as the Operations Director.

Her new responsibilities now include making administrative decisions, payroll, prioritizing expense accounts, and supervising the entire operations aspect of three Autism Academy locations.

"Most importantly, we want this to be a positive place to learn and work," Durant said. "Considering the challenges our teachers already deal with, it's important that they have the necessary resources in the classroom."

Smiling staff, children with autism learning in comfortably contained classrooms, and a professional work environment defines how each site operates at a glance.

"It's always been 'kids first' since I've worked with Laura (Newcomb)," said Durant. "So, it trickles down."

According to Durant, parents are the strongest advocate for their children. With one college graduate, and three college students, the proud mom of four is embracing her purpose of helping others make decisions best suitable for keeping kids first.

Autism is the fastest growing developmental disorder, yet the most underfunded.

Quick Facts

Information provided by the CDC
THE AUTISM ACADEMY
For Education and Development

PROBLEMS ARE NOT FAILURES

Benefits of Robotics for Critical Thinking

AUTISM ACADEMY – An innovative introductory Robotics course is motivating middle and high school students to think critically.

The Autism Academy in Tempe offers rigorous and challenging classes that best benefit students beyond the borders of the classroom.

Robotics and Computer Coding teacher Justin Cothrum is teaching students the importance of strategizing, teamwork, and critical thinking.

Cothrum creates a positive learning environment by inspiring and engaging students while walking the entire class through every step of the process.

"It's going to take a lot of thinking," he said. "So, be patient."

Robotics is a branch of engineering that involves the conception, design, manufacture, and operation of robots.

This field overlaps with electronics, computer science, artificial intelligence, mechatronics, nanotechnology and bioengineering.

"Basically, robotics is a series of steps followed to solve a problem," Cothrum explained.

Robotics is currently an optional class offered at the Autism Academy in Tempe.

Cothrum defined robotics as technology that is used to design, build, and operate robots.

"Everybody thinks differently," he said. "So, we have to be open-minded and respect one another's ideas.

The hands-on experience captivated a classroom of 9 boys with Autism Spectrum

Disorder working together as engineering teammates.

"There are 3 steps to the process," Cothrum said. "1. Think, 2. Do, and 3. Test."

The students partnered together creating multiple think tanks within the classroom.

Afterward, groups assembling robots gain assistance from the robotics and coding teacher and paraprofessionals.

"If it works our problem is solved," said Cothrum.

"If not, then what," he asked?

Students belted out the correct answer in excitement, "Start over at step 1."

The students were given the assignment to design robots able to throw balls.

Class participants are allowed unlimited chances to start over at step one.

"Problems are not failures," Cothrum said.

Repeatedly, he encouraged students to keep creating and thinking critically.

"Great job," "good thinking," and "just try it," were just a few phrases he used to keep students on task.

English Language Arts teacher Tyler Knowles says Cothrum has an exceptional connection with the students throughout the school.

"Robotics is one of the most popular courses for boys," Knowles explained. "And they have a great relationship with Mr. Justin."

Students learned the importance of structural engineering which include mechanisms, motor loading, gear ratio basics, drive trains and object manipulators.

"What if we put the motor on top," one student asked? "Would we have more power and torque?"

Again Cothrum replied, "Try it."

The Autism Academy in Tempe is exposing students to useful problem solving techniques utilizing innovative strategies.

With raised hands, questions echoing around the room, and responsive dialog amongst critical thinkers, the robotics and coding class is a success.

There is no blood test, no scan, and no image that can detect autism. Diagnosis relies on behavioral observation and screening.

Quick Facts

Information provided by the CDC &
THE AUTISM ACADEMY
For Education and Development

RECIPES THAT WORK

Awesome Despite Autism

AUTISM ACADEMY – News is spreading, lines are getting longer daily, and 16 employees at a new Gilbert restaurant are changing the way people see autism.

"Not Your Typical Deli" is operated by 16 employees with autism, and good news is steadily spreading about the cleanliness, professionalism and grommet sandwiches.

Chef W Rieth and his wife, chef Vanessa Luna catered lunches for the Autism Academy prior to taking on this new endeavor.

Now the chef couple has the ingredients to help students with autism transitioning toward independence.

They've partnered with Chuck and Pam DePalma as owners of the new deli.

The DePalma's son Daniel has autism and is also an employee at the restaurant.

The employment opportunity is a 12-week training program equipping people with autism to secure substantial and gainful employment.

"This is a business," said Chef W. "We give them what they need to succeed, and then we push them."

Every employee understands their role, responsibilities, and the importance of building great relationships with every customer.

"This is how they will gain their independence," Chef W said. "And we pay competitive wages."

The Department of Labor enforces the "commensurate wage rate" that allow employers to pay individuals with disabilities at a rate less than minimum wage.

Despite labor allowances, "Not Your Typical Deli" pay workers fair and competitive wages.

The owners created a state-of-the-art gourmet concept that's attracts repeat and new customers. The kitchen has an Ecolab industrial dishwasher complete with a wall monitor that provides repetitive digital video training for employees.

Fresh meats are imported from Italy, and Capistrano's Bakery in Phoenix prepares fresh bread and pastries.

Upon entering, Sam Irving greets guests with a warm welcome.

"Hi, welcome to Not Your Typical Deli," he says while smiling and shaking hands with every guest. "What is your name?"

Irving is 27-years-old, this is his first job, and he is autistic.

Canvass paintings by Irving and Daniel are displayed in the dining area.

For many, the cozy restaurant is the new go-to spot for fresh deli sandwiches and a comfortable uplifting environment.

It is also a melting pot for families supporting loved ones with autism.

The atmosphere echoes with positive energy, "Oh my gosh, this is like an answer to prayer," and "Hi Sam, I remember you, I was hear last week."

Cashier Cordell Sherwood, 19, says this is also his first job.

"I have Asperger's, it's a high functioning form of autism," he said. "I used to be a train wreck. I didn't know how to talk to people, I had serious meltdowns, and I had bad social anxiety."

These days, Sherwood's professionalism is what guests remember about him most.

"Transition is scary for everyone," he said. "Autism or not, change can be scary."

The chefs are patiently working one-on-one with employees and helping them to conquer the fear of transitioning.

"Not Your Typical Deli" is cooking up recipes for success and working to prove that employees are awesome despite autism.

Co-morbid conditions often associated with autism include Fragile X, allergies, asthma, epilepsy, bowel disease, gastrointestinal/digestive disorders, persistent viral infections, PANDAS, feeding disorders, anxiety disorder, bipolar disorder, ADHD, Tourette Syndrome, OCD, sensory integration dysfunction, sleeping disorders, immune disorders, autoimmune disorders, and neuro-inflammation.

Quick Facts

Information provided by the CDC &
THE AUTISM ACADEMY
For Education and Development

TEACHING WITH TECHNOLOGY
Using Tech Tools Without Losing Sight of General Goals

AUTISM ACADEMY – Special needs educators at Tempe Autism Academy are using podcast, robotics, coding, typing, MobyMax, and computers to advance instructional objectives.

Classroom technology at Autism Academy campuses encompass all kinds of tools, including PCI reading and math for students with special needs.

The use of technology is expected to prepare students for the future.

The term "technology" refers to advancement in the approaches used to solve problems or achieve a goal.

Technology has the potential to help students overcome learning deficiencies.

Students naturally gravitate to technology.

From video games to cellular phones and surface pads, children enjoy navigating tech tools.

Students who are autistic work well in solidarity, they stay on task, and identify errors well.

The things that others ordinarily miss they seem to catch.

These attributes motivate teachers to help students with autism explore their extraordinary traits in technology.

Whenever schools are innovative, there will be FUD.

FUD is "fear, uncertainty, and doubt."

However, educators must remain forward thinking.

These emotions usually spiral from individuals who aren't familiar with, or those who are intimidated by the use of technology.

According to Autism Academy development director Shannon Mitchell, more technology is an innovative approach of increasing school services in our modern society.

"Slowly increasing technology enables students to do more research, collaborate on projects, and gather information more quickly. Mitchell said. "We want our students to learn the basics, so we are giving them exposure."

She says, technology is their future.

MobyMax is software used to find and fix learning gaps.

It enables teachers to go slow in order to go fast.

The Autism Academy using this to teacher core foundational skills.

They specialize on identifying strengths and weaknesses to help students transition beyond high school.

In addition to technology, the specialty school recently implemented the *explorer program*.

This enables youth with special needs to explore various electives like cooking, coding, robotics, and much more.

The Autism Academy is soaring above the competition with cutting-edge strategies and a well-balanced curriculum.

A 2008 Danish Study found that the mortality risk among those with autism was nearly twice that of the general population.

Quick Facts

Information provided by the CDC &
THE AUTISM ACADEMY
For Education and Development

NOT YOUR TYPICAL TRANSITION

Entering the Workforce with Autism

AUTISM ACADEMY – More than 3.5 million Americans living with autism are learning to transition into mainstream jobs.

With no uncertainty, like most teenagers, they face countless challenges struggling to shift toward independent living and employment.

The progression from early childhood to independent living with autism is like piecing together a complicated puzzle.

Parents aim to remain optimistic throughout the process. Gilbert resident Renata Irving is a single-mom of two adult sons, one with autism and the other without.

Both are faced with the life-skill goal of making a smooth transition into the workforce.

According to Irvin, who backs both her sons, stereotypes about autism causes a not so typical transition for one.

"All I used to hear is 'there's something wrong with your baby,'" she said. "Or people would say 'there's nothing with him."

In 1994, her oldest son, Sam Irving, 27, was diagnosed with what was then a rare condition called autism.

Twenty-two-years later, the number of children born with autism has increased tremendously. According to the CDC, one in 68 children are diagnosed with some form of autism.

Schools make accommodations, new legislation passes, and research advances, but the puzzle remains challenging.

Public school programs lack consistency, students with autism often get bullied, mistreated, and overlooked, and many parents are consistently fighting for change.

As a result, specialty schools craft curriculums for students with autism only, enabling them to soar in a safe environment.

The Autism Academy for Education and Development operate specialty campuses in Gilbert, Tempe, and Peoria, educating nearly 300 students.

School transition specialist Karen Durst is helping high school students transition smoothly after graduation from the Autism Academy.

The transition team is targeting daily living, technology, and employment skills amongst a host of other training and curriculum preparations.

Durst is avoiding the unnecessary labor of reinventing a new transition curriculum.

"We're just creating a curriculum map to illustrate the big picture of how we get there," she said. "Currently, we're learning their interests and desires."

Transitioning students with autism into the workforce is not a typical task, but some supporters in the autism community have proven unlimited possibilities.

Both Irving's sons recently landed jobs in Gilbert at "*Not Your Typical Deli.*"

The new restaurant is partnering with the autism community with hands-on training that produces real wages.

Autism defines the different between the Irving brothers, but they've mapped a similar journey into the mainstream workforce.

Autism is treatable, it is not a hopeless condition.

Quick Facts

Information provided by the CDC
THE AUTISM ACADEMY
For Education and Development

TURNING HELP INTO HOPE

Autism Twists and Turns

AUTISM ACADEMY – The upward journey from adolescence to adulthood is crammed with unexpected twists and turns.

Most parents feel a sense of anxiety, uncertainty, and frustration about helping their children with autism transition.

For caregivers of children with autism a multitude of undetected and mixed emotions evolve into feelings of fear about the future.

This fear stirs a sea of daunting questions that causes parents to feel like they are drowning in doubt. "Will my child be able to manage without me?" "Will she be able to drive?"

"Will he be able to work?" These are just a few questions parents of people

with autism wrestle with daily while navigating through life's unexpected lane changes.

According to the Autism Consortium, caregivers are most helpful maneuvering their children to self-supervision by seeking answers to optimistic questions.

The Autism Consortium encourages parents to ask questions like, "What makes my child happy," and "What are his strengths?" "What obstacles do she have and what skills are needed to face them?"

These questions serve as headlamps to a brighter and more hopeful future.

The journey to successfully transitioning to independent living is not an uncharted roadmap.

Many parents have experienced success with creative thinking, because all children with autism have different personalities and circumstances.

Avoid navigating the journey alone – help is available.

The Autism Academy for Education and Development is engaging students and families with strategies to navigate from A-to-Z.

The school's mission includes equipping autism students with the necessary components to achieve academically and socially with strong character values.

There are many pieces to the puzzle that starts with enrollment and continues throughout transition. Currently, transition specialist Karen Durst is targeting 11th and 12th graders for college and workforce preparation.

"Parents know their kids better than anyone else," she said. "That's why we're working with campus disability coordinators, teachers, and parents.

The Autism Academy owner Laura Newcomb has invested 4-years strategically assembling a passionate team of teachers and support staff.

Together, the Tempe, Gilbert, and Peoria campuses are providing resources, information, and services needed throughout the autism community.

The Autism Academy is a huge piece of hope in a complicated puzzle with many pieces.

This series of 2016 Autism Academy Reader- Focused-Writing blogs will help bridge families together within the autism community.

The blog will also inform, celebrate, raise awareness, and serve as a literary source to an ever-growing puzzle.

The Autism Academy is helping students and families navigate successfully by turning help into a strong sense of undying hope.

Autism impacts the normal development of the brain in the areas of social interaction, communication skills, and cognitive function. Individuals with autism typically have difficulties in verbal and non-verbal communication, social interactions, and leisure or play activities.

Quick Facts

Information provided by the CDC &
THE AUTISM ACADEMY
For Education and Development

COUNT YOUR BLESSINGS

New Movie Unveils Autism as Heroism

AUTISM ACADEMY – The Thanksgiving season is a great time for family fun, dessert indulging, a movie matinée and expressing gratitude for all good things.

Well, if you're looking for an action packed holiday movie laced with some intriguing content about autism, keep reading.

Recently released blockbuster, "The Accountant" starring Ben Affleck has grossed over $138 million – and counting.

The action thriller gives people with autism a super hero, but consider yourself warned, the movie is R-rated because of its violent content.

The movie plot is like a puzzle, centered on corporate crime and body counts, but outlined in autism transforming into heroism.

Screen writer Bill Dubuque, embedded a strong and supernatural sense of autistic valor into the movie.

He also unveiled the psychological and social battle of people with autism, but he celebrated it as bravery.

Dubuque daringly painted the autism community with broad strokes and imagery defining autism as an X-men style of sci-fi characters.

In effort to remain respectful and accountable to readers of the Autism Academy Blog, we take a journalistic approach.

Professional journalists stick with facts and objectivity, avoiding personal opinion. Unless of course, we are inspired to write an editorial.

Consider this blog an editorial.

The movie left a lot to the imagination.

Could we possibly be undermining the potential powers of people with autism?

Without question, an autistic mind possesses a sense of untapped brilliance and genius.

The movie did two things poorly and irresponsibly.

Producers failed to give proceeds toward research and support of autism, and it diminishes the supernatural role that mothers play in this community everyday.

Whether fact or fiction, Dubuque illustrates that autism super strength is created when fathers are present to challenge their children.

Sounds thrilling for dads, but truth is, there are some pretty amazing moms committed to motivating their kids – and doing so daily.

Unlike the tragedy of absent fathers, abandoning newly diagnosed children with autism, parental roles were reversed in "The Accountant."

The son with autism, Christian Wolff (Ben Affleck) became a mathematics savant with more affinity for numbers than people.

As a CPA, he makes his living as a freelance accountant for dangerous criminal organizations.

He takes on a state-of-the-art robotics company as a legitimate client.

As Wolff gets closer to the truth about a $60 million discrepancy, the body count rises as he rescues the innocent.

Sounds like an ordinary suspense flick with organized crime, killing and conspiracy, but it's not.

The film focuses on sensory, stemming, behavior, isolation, fixation, nonverbal queues and extreme intelligence of people with autism.

With no uncertainty children with autism have untapped superhuman abilities, and for this, parents ought to be thankful.

After counting your many blessings and stuffing your belly with Thanksgiving dinner and dessert, go see The Accountant.

Afterward, perhaps you'll view autism as heroism, too.

At the Autism Academy for Education and Development we believe every child is exception.

Quick Facts

Information provided by the CDC &
THE AUTISM ACADEMY
For Education and Development

NEW PRINCIPAL COMPLETES PUZZLE

*Autism Academy in Position to
Make Headlines in 2017*

AUTISM ACADEMY – The Autism Academy in Tempe recently welcomed a new principal that comes highly recommended with referrals, education, national experience, and countless news headlines.

Dr. Robert Rossi comes with more than high hopes, dreams, and ambitions, he has over 4 decades of leadership in education.

His passion for educating kids and motivating teachers is highlighted in countless newspapers nationwide.

Headlines like "Close the Gap," "Hired to Make Tough Changes," "Educational Reform," and "Road to Rigor" highlight his career of success.

He's been called a "mover and shaker."

Dr. Rossi recently failed at retirement and joined the leadership team at Autism Academy.

He will continue to foster the rich learning environment of the junior high and high schools, while continuing to place strong emphasis on accommodating special needs.

He says he has high expectations and a great respect for the success experienced by the school's owner, Laura Newcomb.

Dr. Rossi's highlight reel also includes teaching college courses in School Administration, Teacher Development, and School Counseling.

He is 1 of 25 leaders in education selected as a state trainer for Breaking Ranks Leading Strategies for Reform.

As an educational consultant, Dr. Rossi emphasizes conscious leadership, energy allocation, and influence works hand in hand.

He says conscious leadership is important, which involves being responsible, building relationships, identifying the superstars, and much more.

"Energy allocation has to do with time, resources, and doing the work once," he explained. "Influence is impacting the thoughts, feelings, and behaviors of others."

The Autism Academy leadership team welcomed Dr. Rossi with open arms as an important piece of the puzzle for the school administration.

Students, teachers, and staff are all prepared to march in sync with Dr. Rossi to their 2017 headlines boasting, "Autism Academy Educating Exceptionally High Achievers."

Great administrators can inspire change and passionate learning while poor ones can destroy a school's culture and burn teachers out.

Quick Facts

Information provided by the CDC &
THE AUTISM ACADEMY
For Education and Development

PAWS FOR THE CAUSE

Autism Academy Service Dogs
Barking Up the Right Tree

AUTISM ACADEMY – It's common for kids to get pets for Christmas, but students at the Autism Academy have six dogs as classmates.

Throughout the school year, each campus shares an extraordinary relationship with six witty and adorable dogs.

"The kids get so excited when they see the dogs," said human resource generalist Lorie Crabtree who provides pet services at the Autism Academy.

"It's very cute."

Dogs help children with autism experiencing sleep conditions, the dangerous tendency of wandering, positive touch, and friendship. In fact, there's a host of benefits to having a dog as a classmate and a friend.

Children with disabilities can pose distinctive challenges for parents.

Autism presents even more distinct challenges than other predominant disabilities.

Children with Autism do not connect well in various environments.

Autism manifests itself most strikingly as impairments in communication and social relationships.

Many children with Autism are nonverbal, and those that are verbal, usually do not use their communication skills to engage with people in their environment.

Some children even exhibit serious behavioral concerns, including, at times, self-injury.

In addition, many of these children have a strong need for structured, routine environments, because change creates feelings of fear and anxiety.

Children with autism are extremely systematic, orderly, and routine oriented.

Disruptive events that occur as minor incidents can cause an extreme breakdown amongst students with autism.

Dogs can help calm, console and distract them from such disappointments.

Service dogs also attract kids that are eager to connect with an outside world that might not understand them.

However, service dogs are expensive.

An estimate for one trained dog is upward of $14,000, depending on the needs.

After the purchase, it takes approximately nine-months of training before the new dog is prepared to fully function in the classroom.

Crabtree is a volunteer puppy trainer for *Guide Dogs for the Dessert* – she's been training dogs for more than a decade.

In addition, she owns *Fur-Ever Chins*, with the help of her husband, Jason.

Their residence is home to 9 dogs and more than 60 chinchillas.

"I've always loved animals," Crabtree said.

"With no plans of having babies of my own, at age 35, I got pregnant," she explained.

After giving birth to her daughter, Meikayla, she acquired a special passion for children.

Crabtree volunteers her weekly pet services at the Autism Academy.

It's called, *"Dog Time."*

On every campus she takes six service dogs into various classrooms.

Mozzie is a 4-year old collie; Kodabear is a 6-year-old new foundland/ leonberger; Sunset is a 7-year-old golden retriever; Willow is an 11-month-old maltipoo; Patriot is a 6-month-old newfoundland; and Rebel is a 6-month-old great pyrenees/anatolian shepherd.

"These service dogs are trained to work specifically with the kids at the school," Crabtree said.

They aid non-verbal students by responding to hand commands.

They support speech therapy by responding to verbal commands.

They assist with field trips by preventing students from straying off.

They help kids remember hygiene techniques.

Crabtree explained, "There are countless services we provide with the dogs."

Teachers also use *Dog Time* as a way to reward students with more personal interaction, dog races, and fetch time.

"A lot of them have personal pets," Crabtree said. "And others are learning to conquer their fear of dogs."

Students transition from fear to calmness as they gain more familiarity with the dogs in a learning environment.

Crabtree said, "We can look back and see the fruits of labor."

DID YOU KNOW

National Dog Day has two goals, to honor dogs, and rescue them from homelessness and abuse. Start early by making plans and personal videos throughout the year to post on online in effort to celebrate National Dog Day, Saturday August 26, 2017. The National Dog Day Foundation hopes to rescue 10,000 dogs a year.

Quick Facts

Information provided by the CDC &
THE AUTISM ACADEMY
For Education and Development

EMPOWERMENT ZONE
The Future of Children with Autism

AUTISM ACADEMY – Seamlessly overlapping responsibilities is how the Autism Academy is empowering kids to shape their own future.

Transition specialist Karen Durst targets higher functioning 11th and 12th graders for college and career preparation.

"I put things on paper and make connections, Durst explained. "But Leslie is the implementer."

Life skills teacher Leslie Dillie works hands-on with students, helping them prepare for a life of independence.

"We're a team," Durst said. "And she's amazing – I couldn't do what she does."

STUDENTS WITH AUTISM LEARNING TO TRANSITION

All people, including children with autism, routinely change from one activity to another.

Whether at home, school, or in the workplace, transitions naturally occur.

These changes happen frequently, causing unexpected stops, activity shifts, and starting new task.

Individuals with autism have greater difficulty shifting attention from one task to another.

The Autism Academy anticipates the need for predictability, eliminates the anxiety that comes with the unexpected, and teaches kids how to plan for disruptions.

When transition strategies are used individuals with autism excel. Students work faster, produce appropriate behavior, and rely less on adult prompting.

There are many transition strategies.

Techniques range from preparation, visual countdown, and photos, to transition cards, and much more.

Various strategies increase predictability.

Hence, high school students at the Autism Academy participate more successfully during school and community outings.

HIGH SCHOOL STUDENTS SUCCESSFULLY LEARNING LIFE SKILLS

"Our on-campus *life skills class* offers students the necessary training to participate in the community," Dillie said.

The program is a cutting edge empowerment zone transforming lives.

During the *life skills class*, students rotate through different work stations learning various office, janitorial, and cooking skills.

"Life skills students make their own paper and organic cleaning wipes," she explained.

Instead of using harsh chemicals, class participants use apple cider vinegar, essential oil, and dish soap as ingredients for Do-It-Yourself cleaning supplies.

Students work independently, sorting through mail, removing staples, shredding and recycling paper.

"They create office labels," Dillie said. "They also file documents based on colors and alphabetically."

During life skills cooking class, students grocery shop weekly, prepare hot lunches, and open "The Grub Hub" every Friday.

Teachers purchase $5 lunches from the life skills program – profits replenish resources needed to fund the Dillie dollar treasure box.

Dillie dollars is class revenue that can be used to purchase meals at McDonald's, DVD movies, Walmart gift cards, snacks and much more.

Life skills participants are eligible for 3 separate off-campus volunteer jobs where students earn experience and Dillie dollars.

The off-campus employment sites include the Community Garden, Not Your Typical Deli, and Tribal Crossfit.

"Every Wednesday the kids travel to their own organic garden," Dillie said. "It's in the Agritopia community of Gilbert.

The agricultural employment experience exposes teenagers to weed picking, seed planting, raking, shoveling, and various gardening techniques.

Dillie says the organic herbs will be used at Not Your Typical Deli.

"On Thursdays, selected students are transported to work at Not Your Typical Deli," she said.

Monday morning workdays consist of vacuuming, mopping, and cleaning exercise equipment at Tribal Crossfit in Chandler.

After working at each off-campus job site, one student decided to gain some entrepreneurial experience.

Cameron, an 18-year-old student, negotiated janitorial deals in order to earn money to purchase holiday gifts.

The Autism Academy is successfully redefining what the future of children with autism looks like by empowering kids to live independently.

A lot of people don't realize that autism is a gift.

Quick Facts

Information provided by the CDC &
THE AUTISM ACADEMY
For Education and Development

www.ingramcontent.com/pod-product-compliance
Lightning Source LLC
Chambersburg PA
CBHW071637050426
42443CB00028B/3392